I0528395

Review Tales
A Book Magazine For Indie Authors

COPYRIGHT © 2024
Review Tales Magazine - A Book Magazine for Indie Authors
This magazine may not be reproduced,
either in part or in its entirety, in any
form, by any means, without written
permission from the publisher, with the
exception of brief excerpts for purposes
of radio, television, or published reviews.
Although all possible means have been
taken to ensure the accuracy of the
material presented, Review Tales is not
liable for any misinterpretation,
misapplication or typographical errors.
All rights, including the right of translation,
are reserved.

Founder & Editor in Chief: S. Jeyran Main
Publisher: Review Tales Publishing & Editing Services
Print & Distribution: Ingram Spark
Cover Design: Moldy Designs
Designs: Pexels
ISBN 978-1-988680-42-2 (Paperback)
ISBN 978-1-988680-41-5 (Digital)
www.jeyranmain.com
For all inquiries please contact us directly.

Contributors

John Edwards
Robert Leet
Bill Hemmig
Andri E. Elia
Mark Morton
Patrick Greenwood
Gregory G. Allen
Gretchen McCullough
Nir Yaniv
Margaret Montet
Teri M Brown
Dan Flanigan
Hal Taylor
L.C. Lewis
Kelly Stone Gamble
Dennis R Bourret and Sam Huynh
Linnea Tanner
Ian P. Eviston
Dr. Colleen Huber
Howard Wolk, John Landry
Thomas Richard Spradlin
Ali Master
Lee Durham Stone
Steve Ramirez
Donna D. Conrad
Dr. Katherine Hutchinson-Hayes

www.jeyranmain.com

Editor's Note

Dear Readers,

As the blossoms of Spring unfold their petals to the warming sun, we are thrilled to present to you the 10th edition of Review Tales Magazine. This issue marks a significant milestone in our journey, and it is with immense gratitude that I extend my heartfelt thanks to each one of you who has supported us along the way.

In this edition, as always, we bring you a carefully curated selection of book reviews, insightful interviews with authors, inspiring words of wisdom, and the much-loved segment of author confessions. Each page is a tribute to the enduring power of words and the transformative experience of reading.

Reflecting on the journey of Review Tales Magazine, it is astounding to see how far we have come. From a modest beginning to reaching this 10th edition, it's been a path filled with learning, growth, and an unwavering passion for books. This accomplishment would not have been possible without the support of our readers, contributors, authors, and the entire literary community. Your encouragement, feedback, and engagement have been the guiding stars of our voyage.

I am particularly grateful to the authors who have shared their stories and experiences with us. Your journeys, challenges, and triumphs have not only enriched our content but have also been a source of inspiration to our readers and aspiring writers. Your willingness to open up in our interviews and confessions sections adds a unique depth and authenticity to our magazine.

To our reviewers, your keen insights and honest critiques are what make this magazine a trusted source for book lovers everywhere. Your dedication to exploring new genres and uncovering hidden gems in the literary world is commendable.

As we celebrate this 10th edition, it is also a time to look ahead. We are committed to continuously improving and expanding our content to bring you the most engaging and diverse literary experiences. Our goal remains to create a platform where readers and writers can connect, discover, and be inspired.

In closing, I invite you to dive into the pages of our Spring Edition. Whether you're in search of your next great read, seeking writing tips from successful authors, or simply looking to lose yourself in the world of books, there's something in here for everyone.

Thank you once again for being part of our journey. Here's to many more editions filled with the magic of books!

With warm regards,

Jeyran Main

Editor-in-Chief
Review Tales Magazine

A Project of a Lifetime
by John Edwards

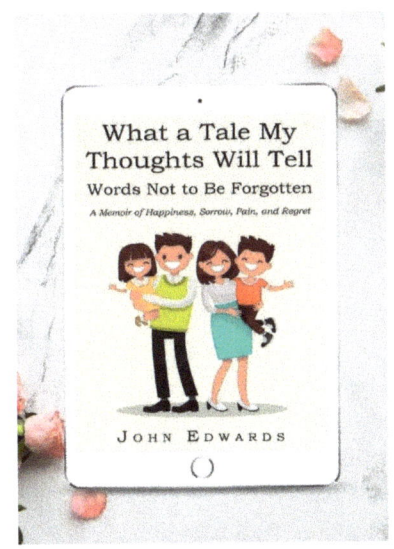

I began writing my memoir after retiring from United Parcel Service and the unforeseen end of my second management career with Enterprise Holdings Inc. in Roseville, California. At sixty-eight years of age, having completed thirteen years of service with this exceptional organization, I planned to devote another seven years to achieve a twenty-year career and retire at age seventy-five to match my father's work-life commitment. However, the ending of my career at Enterprise was bittersweet as the World Health Organization announced the spread of a mysterious coronavirus-related pneumonia in Wuhan, China, in January 2020.

President Trump declared COVID-19 a national emergency by March, and the NBA had indefinitely suspended their season. In April, I accepted a voluntary buyout as Enterprise battled the financial turbulence caused by the virus. As pandemic lockdowns began and virtual medical appointments became standard, transitioning into an isolated lifestyle was recommended.

During this time, the virus was unprecedented, causing fear and anxiety. However, I found this time a welcoming break from my hyperconnected life, feeling comfortable with the prospect of isolating for an extended period. Seclusion became an interval of restoration, reflection, and self-evaluation. I reflected on my life, which deepened my appreciation of my life's successes and failures. Self-reflecting on the lessons learned from failed marriages and family estrangement helped me realize my role in the cause and effect of dissolution. Being socially isolated started my journey into renewal and seeking meaning through personal contemplation. My inspiration for writing a book began. It is a story of where I came from, what hopes and dreams I fought for, and what single dynamic is most important regarding the true meaning of life. It's the story of my life. This novel unveils the influence of cultural, psychological, and sociological factors that influence and shape our identity.

A literary work of happiness, sorrow, pain, and regret began. Over the last two years, while grappling to find the right words to put on the pages, what I didn't anticipate through creating and completing the task of writing a book about my life was how it led me to discover the true meaning of life. It was quite literally a project of a lifetime. I wanted to keep my story and legacy alive. It is a gift to my family and future generations. My memoir is about sharing emotions and turning my written words into wisdom gained. Sharing these experiences will hopefully benefit and provide insights to readers who might find themselves in similar circumstances.

John Edwards grew up in the small Bay Area bedroom community of San Lorenzo, California, a twin son of a Korean War veteran turned patternmaker for the Alameda Naval Air Station. After a school career that included St. Joachim's Catholic, Arroyo High School, Chabot College, and the prestigious St. Mary's College of California, he married young, at twenty-six, and settled in Martinez, California.

Curosity
by Robert Leet

My first foray into science was a failure. I left MIT as an undergraduate after two years, confused and unhappy with myself and the education system, but I needed to continue in school to avoid the University of Saigon, which I termed the Vietnam War. I changed my major to English because I realized I would never need to take a test again in school, just write. I soon began writing poetry and short stories and even published a few in obscure journals. I loved writing, and I still feel some of my poems are pretty good, but I realized the concentration required would make it hard for me to make a living, and I was not interested in the world or culture of literature at the time.

I spent a decade and a half exploring life and then went back to school to study engineering, this time with more success than as a teenager. At some point, I quit writing poetry, or perhaps I should say I began working in the poetry of mathematics. As I work for myself, I can pretty much write when I want, and breaking all the advice of accomplished writers, I write from inspiration. If I have latched onto an idea I wish to convey, I may write for days, ignoring other work.

Then, I may take a break for weeks or months to wrestle with my thoughts. I think this method is necessitated by using mathematical concepts that need consistent yet clear, and it takes time to give them shape.

I know that mathematics and science are a turn-off for some people, but, like CP Snow, I have always rejected studying the humanities or the sciences. True curiosity demands that we explore both, and I cannot imagine my existence without curiosity.

Resonant describes the attempts of a mostly retired mathematician and his coterie of friends to decipher the language of humpback whales, mostly against the wishes of the U.S. Navy, and even the whales themselves. It also delves into the nature of how whales can measure time or distance in a liquid world, and how that relates to how our human perspective came to be dominated by counting and measurement.

Robert Leet is a self-employed structural engineer living and working in a rural part of New England. He felt as though he could write a book as the last person who really remembers the United States before the Interstate Highway system, as he used to travel with his dad, an independent truck driver, during summers throughout the 1950s. He thinks that experience gave him a Whitmanesque feel for this country (and the world) he has never relinquished.

A WRITER'S SPLIT PERSONALITY
by Bill Hemmig

My first short story collection, Americana: Stories, was published last summer, and I've gotten swept up in the publisher's marketing campaigns—blog posts (text and video), podcasts, interviews, reviews, and articles like this one. Like most writers, I have a full-time job that pays the bills, so now I have two full careers. And I still need to find time to work on my next collection! Here's what I learned very quickly about balancing two careers and a life:

·I can't wait for the muse to strike. I've always grabbed my writing time in the evenings, on weekends, and on holidays, and now the same time must also be devoted to promotional activities. When I have time to write, I must sit down and write, whether the inspiration fairy has joined me. Self-discipline is everything.

·I must remember to have a life. Like many writers, I'm an introvert. By day, I'm an administrator in higher education, and I've developed an extroverted, introverted personality to function in my job. Therefore, when I'm not at my job the temptation is to throw off the extroverted introvert and hunker down in my house with no one but my cat. Unless I want the subjects of my stories restricted to higher education administration and cats, I need to make time to get out there, hang with friends, create new ones, go to cultural events, travel, and have the occasional adventure. There's no writing without living.

·I must also remember which of my personalities is the real me. It's straightforward to get caught up in one's day job, especially if one is a professional anything by day. We all need ways to recall which of ourselves is foremost. I have the ISBNs (International Standard Book Numbers) of my two published books tattooed on my left bicep. Not for promotional purposes when I'm at the beach but to remind me of my true identity.

Bill Hemmig is the author of Americana: Stories and Brethren Hollow, both published by Read Furiously. His short stories appear in Read Furiously's Life in the Garden State anthologies, The World Takes and Stay Salty, and in the Toho Publishing anthology, The Best Short Stories of Philadelphia, 2021. He has had stories published in the journals The Madison Review, Philadelphia Stories, and Children, Churches and Daddies (cc&d), and he is a three-time finalist in the New Millennium Writing Awards. By day he is the Dean of the Learning Resources & Online Learning at Bucks County Community College in Pennsylvania.

My Journey and How I Returned to Write
by Mark Morton

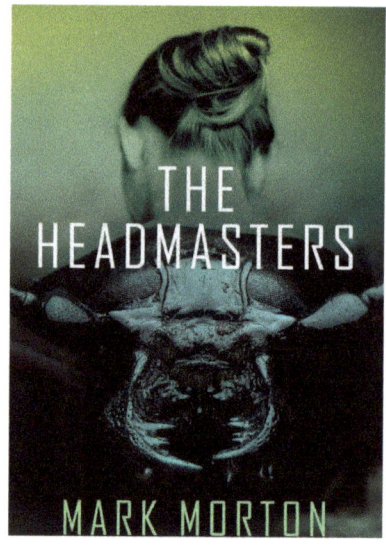

Prior to 2006, I published four books, three of which were very well-received (let's not talk about the other one. Then, I suddenly stopped writing for fifteen years and only returned to it recently. Why the hiatus? Well, my wife and I adopted four older children, all of whom had PTSD from the neglect and/or abuse they experienced before being apprehended by Family and Children's Service. They'd also fallen far behind in school. And one of them had (and has) Asperger Syndrome. So, as you can imagine, these kids needed our unstinting care, support, and love. My wife resigned from her day job, and when I got home from work, our joint attention was on one of the kids or all of the kids, or some subset of the kids, until their bedtime—which was also our bedtime!

As I reread the preceding paragraph, it might sound like I'm complaining. I'm not. Raising our children—helping them overcome the challenges and crap that life had dealt them—was the most meaningful thing my wife and I have ever done. Yes, it was exhausting. Utterly, mind-numbingly and body-achingly exhausting. But we now have four beautiful children who are (most of the time) happy, independent, and confident. And they love us as much as we them. So, of course, we wouldn't change a thing about how our lives have unfolded.

But don't I regret, even a tiny bit, not having those fifteen years to write? Nope. Because I believe I came out of those fifteen years with a perspective and depth of understanding and—dare I say—wisdom that I would never have acquired if I'd spent all that time writing. I would have no doubt written more books. But they wouldn't have been the kind of books that I now admire—the kind of books I now want to write and, I hope, have now written.

So, here's some of that wisdom I claim to have acquired: if you're not writing but you're still doing something you experience as meaningful, that's fine. In fact, it's excellent. Because not only is it meaningful in itself, but it will also, inevitably, make you an even better writer.

Mark Morton, acclaimed for his culinary and linguistic nonfiction, including the Julia Child Award-nominated "Cupboard Love" and the Alexander Isbister Award-winning "The End," has authored three other notable titles and over 50 columns for Gastronomica. His expertise extends to broadcasting, with more than a hundred language and culture segments on CBC Radio. Morton holds a PhD in sixteenth-century literature from the University of Toronto and has an extensive teaching background in France and Canada. Alongside his wife, author Melanie Cameron, he juggles a busy family life with four children and several pets.

Leaving Your Body Behind When Venturing Out to Write
by Patrick Greenwood

Hemingway once wrote, "Writing and travel broaden your ass if not your mind, and I like to write standing up." Becoming a full-time writer has more to do with mental mountain climbing than opening a laptop and beginning the daily routine of pounding on the keyboard.

Getting out of your personal space is one great way to discover your voice. It is easy to jump in the car, head to the beach, or walk around the block. This physical activity either creates a positive writing mindset or this motion brings on a new level of distraction.

Mastering the art of brainstorming and daydreaming may become your favorite creative writing strategy. Leaving your body for a moment just to let the creative fluid take on a life of its own has helped me deliver richer storylines, better character development, and incredible endings. Allowing myself to physically immerse myself in the time to enjoy a quiet departure from the keyboard helps me love my writing.

My favorite place for brainstorming sessions starts with sitting at the beach in Southern California. Watching the sunrise at Laguna Beach at 6:46 local time is an event, never duplicated. Beachgoers who see sunrises and sunsets claim that each event is always different. As in writing, we often try to be authentic and unique. Sometimes, all we need to do is close our eyes and imagine the sun coming up, the raindrops hitting the roof, or hearing people talk outside.

Loving what you do starts with liking the way you approach your craft. Writing should never be a chore. Yet, when we rely solely on one source for inspiration, we limit our ability to expand our thoughts.

Leaving your body behind and allowing yourself the pleasure of letting your mind find its way will become your most significant content source.

Enjoy the moment and the journey.

After serving in the military, Patrick Greenwood built a 25-year career in information technology, gaining diverse experience across sales, engineering, support, and design. Inspired by his business travels across Asia and Europe, he began writing in 2020, drawing from his cycling trips in various countries. His debut novel, "Sunrise in Saigon," an award-winner on Amazon.com in 2022, incorporates non-fictional events from Vietnam's history. Greenwood's upcoming novel, "The Shores of Okinawa," set for release in May 2024, continues the Jack Kendall series with added intrigue. Besides novel writing, Patrick ghostwrites for cybersecurity firms, blogs, and hosts the award-winning podcast, "Writers on Writers over a triple espresso," live on Wednesdays and Saturdays at 10:00 am PST.

Worldmaker of Yand - Yildun by Andri E. Elia

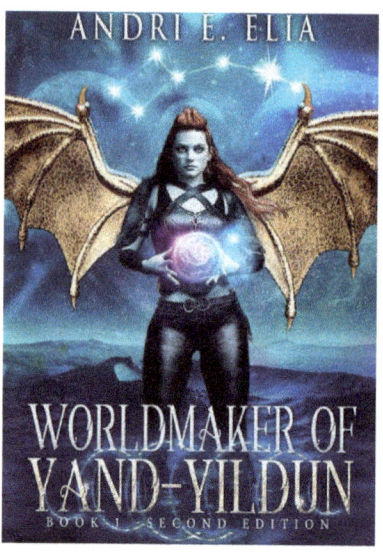

When did you first realize you wanted to be a writer?

I started writing poems in elementary school and wrote my best award-winning work in high school. I began making up stories around that time but didn't start writing them down until I was in college, and I wrote them in English. Ever since then, I have dreamt of becoming a published writer.

What would you say is your interesting writing quirk?

I love to write in first-person narration, especially when I have a character as interesting and dynamic as Yanara. You won't see that in my new book, Queen of Highwings, because I wanted to capture several POVs. So I'm writing Queen mainly in the third person, with one or two passages in the first, for that extra zing.

How did you get your book published?

Ah, the torturous road to publication! First, I thought I needed an agent to find me a traditional publisher and a movie deal(!). I struggled and had a thousand rejections. Well, not that many, but all rejections. Some kindly said that my book was really good but not a good fit. All were form replies. At some point, I thought, how much rejection can I endure? And also, is this really that bad to merit the rejection?

So I entered Yildun and Polaris (its sequel) in Screencraft's Cinematic Book competition—I had not yet completed Eltanin. Can you imagine my surprise when both Yildun and Polaris were Quarterfinalists? Coverfly listed them in the top 18 sci-fi books of 2022, and Polaris is on their Red List this January.

Encouraged by this, I realized that my biggest aspiration was to have my books printed in quality print and read by many people. I received a few perfect editorial reviews, got the books illustrated by a very talented graphics designer, Ms. Dormishev, and self-published on Amazon. I stopped querying agents for now. The quality of Amazon's print books is amazing! It exceeds even this perfectionist's expectations.

Where did you get your information or idea for your book?

I think in images. Several years ago, a persistent vision of a woman kneeling on a frozen lake popped into my mind. Her head was bent, and she hugged herself and rocked back and forth as if crying. When she looked at the sky, red flashes came from her eyes. She was such a lonely, compelling figure! Who was she? I wanted to understand everything about her—why was she alone in that icy desolation? Who/where were her people? Did she have a family? Why was she bathed in darkness? Then she unfurled her wings and "flew" to the moon!

I didn't write Yanara's story until a few years later. I first researched astronomy, where to locate Yanara's world, and how to build it. What kind of a star was her sun, what kind of a planet she lived on, and did it have moons? Then, the science of black holes and wormholes—the way Yanara traverses the universe. Wings and flight patterns with military formations to create the Yandar Flyer Force. Also, warfare strategies, from European Medieval and Chinese Wuxia with swords, bows, and arrows to Space Battles with celestial cannons. When I finally sat down to write Yildun, it took me three months cover-to-cover.

An American Tragedy by Dan Flanigan

When did you first realize you wanted to be a writer?

A freshman in high school. As life moved on, I did a lot of other things instead of that, but it always stayed with me, and I managed to publish my first book many decades later. Since 2019, I have published a book of poetry, a book of short fiction, and three books in the Peter O'Keefe series (An American Tragedy will be the fourth).

How do you schedule your life when you're writing?

It may happen someday, but I am not a full-time writer. I have tried to follow recommendations to write every day and write a certain amount of words, or pages, or whatever. But so far I haven't managed to do that. I describe my process, such as it is, as "manic depressive." But am "blessed" with an unhealthy general work ethic, and the good news is I have still managed to write and publish the last three books in the O'Keefe series in a period of five years despite the drawbacks of my "method."

Where did you get your information or idea for your book?

An American Tragedy is the fourth book in a crime/detective series that begins in 1986, and my intention is to carry O'Keefe and the characters in his orbit through the history of our times. It's the fourth book and I haven't made it past 1988, but the 1980s was quite a decade. I think I will manage to move into the 90s in the next book.

What do you like to do when you're not writing?

I continue to be a practicing lawyer and pursue a wide range of interests from sacred choral music to ballet and modern dance to tennis and kayaking.

How do you process and deal with negative book reviews?

Fortunately, I have not received that many negative ones. When I get them, I try hard to (1) absorb any useful negative criticisms and resolve to do better next time and (2) ignore the stupid or just misguided ones. The hard thing is to "fairly" (without self-deception) distinguish between (1) and (2).

A Fifth of the Story by Dr. Katherine Hutchinson-Hayes

When did you first realize you wanted to be a writer?

As a young child in elementary school, I vividly recall my fascination with the world of literature, theater, and music. I was captivated by the way each of these mediums could weave a story and create a world in which I could immerse myself. It was during this time that I first realized my passion for writing, and the desire to create something magical by combining these three art forms became a driving force in my life. The idea of crafting a story that could transport readers to a different time and place and evoke emotions through the power of language has been a source of inspiration ever since.

How do you schedule your life when you're writing?

As an avid writer, I have developed a disciplined routine that allows me to make steady progress in my projects. I follow a strict schedule that requires me to work on a single chapter every day without fail. By committing to this routine, I ensure that I am consistently making progress towards my goals.

To further motivate myself, I have joined various writing organizations that help keep me accountable. Through these groups, I have access to a community of fellow writers who offer support and encouragement. This helps me stay on track and provides a sense of camaraderie that makes the writing process more enjoyable.

Despite my many other obligations, I make it a point to prioritize my writing project. By dedicating time and attention to my craft, I am not only improving my skills but also honoring my own creativity. Ultimately, my goal is to produce work that is both meaningful and impactful, and I am willing to put in the necessary effort to make that happen.

What would you say is your interesting writing quirk?

A fascinating writing habit that I possess is my love for incorporating soundtracks into my writing process. I find that each writing project demands a particular type of music to set the appropriate tone and mood. Whether it's classical music for a reflective piece or upbeat pop songs for a more energetic and livelier piece, music helps me capture the essence of my writing. Additionally, I like to create a serene ambiance by lighting candles, which helps me focus and relax my mind. Finally, I always make sure to have a steaming hot cup of coffee or tea by my side as it adds a comforting and cozy feeling to my writing process.

How did you get your book published?

For a considerable period, I relentlessly pursued literary agents and submitted numerous inquiries and proposals to various publishing houses. However, what's interesting is that I had someone I'd previously worked with as a freelancer act as a middleman for my novel. Essentially, she played the role of an agent on my behalf. It was because of her efforts and connections that I was able to spark the interest of a publisher who was keen on taking on my project.

The Last Magdalene by Donna D. Conrad

When did you first realize you wanted to be a writer?

When I was a Junior in High School, I took College Prep English with Mr. David Sundstrand. He encouraged me not only to write but to read voraciously. It was his belief in me that made me want to write and made me want to become someone who made a difference in the world. I owe David for kindling my love of literature in general and my love of writing in particular.

How do you schedule your life when you're writing?

I've tried a number of different schedules over the last several years and always come back to starting fresh each morning with the next chapter or scene in the book I'm currently working on. In the afternoon, I work on editing the prior day's writing, promotion, social media posts, and catching up on emails.

Where did you get your information or idea for your book?

I met a Magdalene scholar who told me about the missing books in the New Testament, some attributed to this remarkable woman whose importance and influence had been systematically removed from early church texts and doctrine. But that wasn't enough. The church then slandered and maligned her. I knew her name, Mary Magdalene, but little more than that about her. I was fascinated and dove into research with both feet. I found a plethora of information about her, her life, her teachings, her prominent position with Yeshua bar Yosef (Jesus of Nazareth), and her lasting importance to women throughout the last two millennia.

During my research about Miriam, I found archaeological evidence that goddess worship was still a part of daily life in Jerusalem during the first century. That, combined with the fact that Magda in Hebrew means tower and exalted, led me down the path of finding out all I could about goddess worship during that time.

Is there anything you would like to confess about as an author?

I'm writing historical fiction about women who have been marginalized in history and am obsessed with digging through ancient sources to find even the briefest mention of women before the thirteenth century. So my confession is that if you get me started on women's roles in history, you're in for a long conversation.

How do you process and deal with negative book reviews?

Not every book is for every reader. I realize that my subject matter can trigger deeply held feelings in readers, and so I take negative comments as an expression of that particular reader's personal feelings, not as a reflection on my ability as a writer or on the merit of the story I've written.

The Monsters of Marymount Mansion by Gregory G. Allen

When did you first realize you wanted to be a writer?

My mom would say I was always a storyteller. I would write stories and plays as a kid...sometimes even directing the neighbors in these plays. I guess my love of writing and directing BOTH started at an early age. That love of storytelling carried me through my life.

How do you schedule your life when you're writing?

I'm a juggler, and I work best when I have many projects on my plate. So, writing is one thing I carve out time to do...of course, taking notes on my phone throughout the day when I'm inspired by something.

How did you get your book published?

I've had 11 books published...both kids' books and adult novels. My first kids' books won a contest with MeeGenius Publishing, and then two of those were acquired by Houghton Mifflin Harcourt. I've also worked with several indie publishers and have published on my own. I have my own Indie Media Company, where I've published books (other authors as well as my own) and produced films under that company.

Where did you get your information or idea for your book?

The idea to write my monster book came to me when I was 15, and I wrote a musical about monsters who lived in the basement. All these years later, I felt it was time to turn it into a children's story. I can be inspired by life around me, a story on the news...usually, I write about a person or group who feels different or attacked due to those differences.

What do you like to do when you're not writing?

I love to travel. I've gone all over North America and Europe, and Puerto Vallarta, Mexico, is my happy place.

What was one of the most surprising things you learned in creating your book?

I learn when I really challenge myself...I can do it. I was nervous because I'd never written a chapter of a book. It's much different from a picture book or writing my adult novels. I really do thrive under pressure.

Is there anything you would like to confess about as an author?

I am a terrible speller, and my grammar "ain't so good" either. I would be lost without an editor.

As a child, what did you want to do when you grew up?

I wanted to be a performer and I'm so lucky that I'm still performing on stage and in film. I work in the arts. I do arts management at a theater, so my life has been full of creativity. I'm blessed.

How do you process and deal with negative book reviews?

It's so hard. I can tell you my first novel over ten years ago got amazing reviews, but I can still quote you that one person who was in a mood and gave me a one-star review.

Shahrazad's Gift by Gretchen McCullough

When did you first realize you wanted to be a writer?

I was writing short stories in high school, and I had teachers who encouraged me. But the first person who encouraged me seriously to write was the novelist Jaimy Gordon. I was on a tennis scholarship at Stephen College in 1980. I had intended to sign up for courses in radio and television, but instead, I took a beginning fiction writing course. Quite literally, a single course and the encouragement of one professor pointed me in the direction of fiction. Many other writers have encouraged me: R.V. Cassill, Bob Coover, Allen Wier, John Keeble, and George Garrett. In Cairo, the Egyptian novelist Sonallah Ibrahim encouraged me to write my novel.

How do you schedule your life when you're writing?

The American University in Cairo has granted me many leaves. If you are working on a vast project, you need extensive stretches of time.

If I have a period like this, I typically wake up early and work at my desk until around noon. I play tennis, swim, meet friends, and read in the afternoon.

If you are writing a novel, you must visit the garden daily. I have a desk that looks out over beautiful trees and feels like a tree house. A music college is in front of our building, and sometimes, I am blessed by the sound of a saxophone or the piano. Other times, it will be the noise and shouting of people in the street.

How did you get your book published?

I found my publisher, the late Scott Davis, from an old Syrian friend whom I met on a Fulbright to Syria in the nineties. Cune Press is a boutique press out of Seattle that publishes books on the Middle East. I sent him my novel, Confessions of a Knight Errant, and he sent me a contract three weeks later. I was elated! I had tried for about five years to get it published.

He was so enthusiastic about my work that he wanted to republish my story collection, Shahrazad's Tooth, which was originally published by a small publisher in Cairo. Sadly, Scott died the month my novel was published, October 2022.

His wife, Mary, is publishing Shahrazad's Gift. It is coming out this spring, 2024.

As a child, what did you want to do when you grew up?

I thought I would become a lawyer, like my father and grandfathers. But it didn't work out that way. During college, I spent a few summers working as a receptionist at their law office and thought the work was too dry. I was more interested in the colorful clients who sometimes would appear. Once, some carnival people came to see my Dad. My dad said they would be paying the fee, but I didn't notice the woman carrying a purse. She reached into her rather large brassiere and fished out some cash. This captured my imagination more than the pink time slips or the files that had to be filed in the storage unit.

Shahrazad's Gift by Margaret Montet

When did you first realize you wanted to be a writer?

I have always wanted to be a writer, and I kind of always knew I didn't have to only be a writer. In other words, I could pursue another path (music theory, librarianship, education) and add the writing to whatever career presented itself. It wasn't until middle age that I realized I deserved to throw my energy into writing for fun (travel) and pursue an MFA in Creative Nonfiction.

What would you say is your interesting writing quirk?

I think this is getting to be a quirk: I prefer to write longhand! I have a connection between my creative brain and whatever writing utensil is in my hand. When I eventually type my messy manuscript, I hear it as I type, and this serves as my first revision.

Where did you get your information or idea for your book?

My idea came from traveling to many places, foreign and domestic, with groups, one travel buddy, or solo. I noticed I do much research about the places I intend to visit or at least more than people I know, and I'm inspired to read about the places I've been once I'm home. It occurred to me that other travelers I know don't do this, so I must be some kind of nerd. Hence: Nerd Traveler!

What do you like to do when you're not writing?

I'm a college librarian, and most semesters, I teach a section or two of public speaking or English composition. I also deliver lectures in various lifelong learning venues on topics related to my travels and music background. These don't leave too much time for traveling, quilting, crocheting, or embroidery, but I try to fit those in when I can.

As a child, what did you want to do when you grew up?

Since I started playing the clarinet at age ten, I have wanted to be a music teacher, and specifically, a high school band director, once I became aware of that possibility. Once in college, I remembered I didn't really have much patience with kids, so I switched to music theory and got a master's degree in that. Then I got a Master's in Library Science, thinking I'd like to be a music librarian. I did get to do that for a couple of years, but then found a librarian gig with less "publish-or-perish" stress.

The Good Soldier by Nir Yaniv

When did you first realize you wanted to be a writer?

I've never realized it. Like many other events and turns in my life, it just happened. I first encountered science fiction at an early age at the local library of the small Israeli town I grew up in. Being an avid reader, I finished every sci-fi book they had to offer before hitting 4th grade. There are other genres, too, but I loved sci-fi the most. That's how I became a reader. In my twenties, I found myself a member of the Israeli Society for SF&F. They needed a website, and I volunteered to create it. I've set it as Israel's first online genre magazine. That's how I became an editor. After a while, it occurred to me, as an afterthought, that I could also write my own stories. And viola - a writer was born.

Similar chains of events led to me becoming a musician and a director, but that's - as a much better author once wrote - another story.

What would you say is your interesting writing quirk?

Tempo is of the utmost importance to me. If the text doesn't sing to me in a certain way - it's doomed. I'm also quite particular regarding last words - in a sentence, a paragraph, a story. Notice the second sentence of this very paragraph: I could have started it as "The text is doomed if…" - but I didn't. I wanted "doomed" to be the last word of the sentence. Cause and effect, problem and solution. Music works this way, too, by the way.

Another appetite: applying abundant aggravating, annoying, aberrant alliterations.

Where did you get your information or idea for your book?

Like most Israelis, I served three years in the army. I was lucky enough to be a non-combatant. During that time, I considered myself unique in assessing the incredible stupidity of the system. Imagine my surprise when, a few years later, I encountered books written by other veterans - of different armies and historical periods - and realized that their experiences were much like mine. These were the roots from which, many years later, The Good Soldier would grow.

As I grew older, I noticed that the military science fiction books I loved as a child were quite different from what I remembered. The most notable example was Heinlein's Starship Troopers, which I still like despite strongly disagreeing with its conclusion. Clearly, serving in the army is not required to become a good citizen. This kind of thinking is outright fascism. I could argue longer here, but my novel says it better. Check it out!

What do you like to do when you're not writing?

I create weird animations. I compose and record music in my own studio. Don't get me started on studio equipment. Or cameras. Where was I? Well, I play my bass. I do horrible things with modular synthesizers. Occasionally, to their eternal chagrin, some innocent soul would ask me to edit a story.

An Enemy Like Me by Teri M Brown

How do you schedule your life when you're writing?

I am what I call a binge pantster. This means that not only do I write by the seat of my pants without an outline, but I also write for long stretches of time when the mood hits me. In fact, I wrote the first draft of An Enemy Like Me in two weeks while at a writer's retreat. During that time, I ate easy-to-prepare meals at my desk, forgot to check on my family, and rarely slept. Once I am done writing, I may not pick up a pen again for several days.

What would you say is your interesting writing quirk?

Most authors I've spoken with like to have peace and quiet while writing. Not me! I like to write while real life is going on around me. Doing so keeps me connected with my readers.

How did you get your book published?

I chose to use the hybrid publisher, Atmosphere Press. This gives me the best of both traditional and self-publishing while eliminating many pitfalls. For instance, I got An Enemy Like Me published eight months after acceptance, and the rights to the book belong solely to me as if I had self-published. On the other hand, I had a professional cover designer, editor, and proofreader. It has been a good fit for what I'm trying to accomplish as an author.

Where did you get your information or idea for your book?

An Enemy Like Me is loosely based on my family's history. My family is German-American, and my grandfather fought in WWII in Germany. Although our family has been in the United States since the 1700s, fighting in Germany was unsettling for my grandpa. He once told me, "I always wondered if the person on the other side of my gun was a cousin." That statement became the basis of the novel.

What do you like to do when you're not writing?

I am very eclectic when it comes to activities beyond writing. I enjoy reading, playing word games and board games, ballroom dancing, cycling, swimming, collecting shells on the beach, photography, going to live shows, attending estate sales, playing bridge, and cooking. I'm currently learning to play the piano and have plans to learn to paint with watercolors and play the violin.

What was one of the most surprising things you learned in creating your book?

Most people learned that the United States had internment camps for Japanese Americans during WWII. However, most did not know that there were camps for German-Americans, too. Not everyone of German descent landed in a camp, but if they were suspected of having Nazi leanings or too many connections to the Old Country, they could be taken to a camp.

As a child, what did you want to do when you grew up?

When I was a child, I wanted to be three things: An author, an Olympic ice skater, and a brain surgeon. I'm not sure this was prophetic, however. I am very clumsy and can't do much more than remain upright on skates, and I have a complete distaste for blood, so neither of those would have ever worked out. I think I wanted to be an author because I loved books and read everything I could get my hands on.

FOR A SONG: ILLUSTRATED MUSIC HISTORY

Hal Taylor

Writing about history came to me rather late in life. I suppose it's because the past now looks more inviting than the future. Not that it's a bad thing. History is everywhere; it's a bottomless topic.

My first four books covered the regional history of the Delaware Valley, where I've lived almost forever. But I also had a career as a musician in a previous life and couldn't resist the urge to write about songs that I grew up with, songs that are so deeply embedded in the general consciousness that we tend to take them for granted. And each one has a unique story, like "Greensleeves," a tune so old it has gone through fusion and become two separate songs. And some contain burning questions: Who is this "Danny Boy" we sing about every St. Paddy's Day? Do we salute the flag or have a drink when we hear "The Star Spangled Banner?" Are there actually figs in the figgy pudding?

I chose two dozen of these musical classics, researched extensively, and found answers to most of the questions, while others will forever remain mysteries. As with my previous works, I enhanced the song narratives with my original illustrations, most of which have been inspired by the Golden Age of Illustration art. I also included a bonus chapter describing my own musical career that left much to be desired during the much kinder era of peace, love, and failed dreams.

Over a long and varied career Hal Taylor has been a musician, typographer, type designer, college professor, illustrator, and author. His first four books have focused on Delaware Valley history, including The Illustrated Delaware River, Before Penn, Artifacts, and The Book of Wedges. His latest work, For a Song, explores the origins of two dozen of the most famous songs ever written. All of Hal's books are rich with his original illustrations and well researched narratives. To see reviews and samples of his illustrations as well as direct links to order on Amazon, please visit www.haltaylorillustration.com

For a Song digs into the backgrounds of two dozen of the most popular songs ever written; songs that have remained relevant through the years and become institutions. What surfaces is both fascinating and surprising: from the copyright debacle of "Happy Birthday" to the sad inspiration for "Rudolph the Red Nosed Reindeer." From the grass roots of "Greensleeves" to the futile search for figs in "We Wish You a Merry Christmas." Each tune is thoroughly researched, presented in lively narrative, and lovingly illustrated by the author. It also includes a bonus chapter describing the author's own musical career that left much to be desired, during the era of peace, love, and failed dreams.

SOME PROJECTS CHANGE US

L.C. Lewis

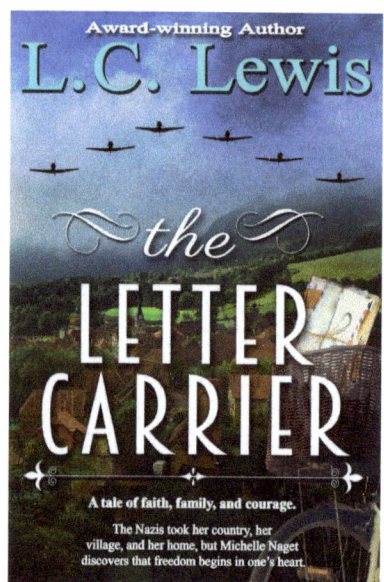

People often ask me where book ideas come from. Truthfully, they arrive in a dozen unexpected ways—from life experiences or a news headline to a location or person that inspires me. My book, The Letter Carrier, was born in such a way. Michelle Naget was a tiny woman sitting in an assisted living center. Her age and French accent prompted me to ask a few questions, and her story began to pour out—a tale of life and death, coercion and occupation, family, faith, and freedom. I spent three years interviewing her before writing her story so her history would not be lost. I had no idea how this project would impact me or the readers of The Letter Carrier, the book it inspired.

In the early days of WWII, the Naget family's attempted flight from France ended in capture. They were forced to turn back and serve the Nazi leadership who'd commandeered their home. The next four years were spent on a razor's edge of Nazi threats, where a word, action, or rejected advance could mean execution. It's impossible to read her story and not experience her fear or witness the Allied heroes' sacrifice through the eyes of a grateful, freed French girl and find words to express adequate gratitude for their heroism.

Michelle's four brothers never spoke of their war years. Their children said reading The Letter Carrier helped them "know" their fathers. After reading Michelle's story, readers felt inspired to learn about and share their own families' WWII stories.

The most important lesson Michelle taught me was that exquisitely challenging experiences don't have to make us hard. During a required move to Germany, empathy won. Past bitterness turned to love as she recognized the mutual suffering the German people experienced during the war. Her empathetic, forgiving heart has been a touchstone to readers.

Meeting Michelle was a gift, but many others of her generation have incredible stories that must be preserved. I hope we begin asking questions and recording the stories before time steals them from us forever.

Laurie Lewis is a RONE Award Winner (The Dragons of Alsace Farm) and was twice named a New Apple Literary Award winner in 2017 (The Dragons of Alsace Farm), and in 2018, winning New Apple Literary's Best New Fiction Award (Love on a Limb.) She is also a BRAGG Medallion honoree, A Readers' Favorite Award Winner, and she was twice named a Whitney Awards and USA Best Books Awards finalist. Her next project, a political suspense novel titled Revenge Never Rests, published by Covenant Communications Inc., is scheduled for an October 2022 release.

BECOMING ONE WITH THE ROCK
Kelly Stone Gamble

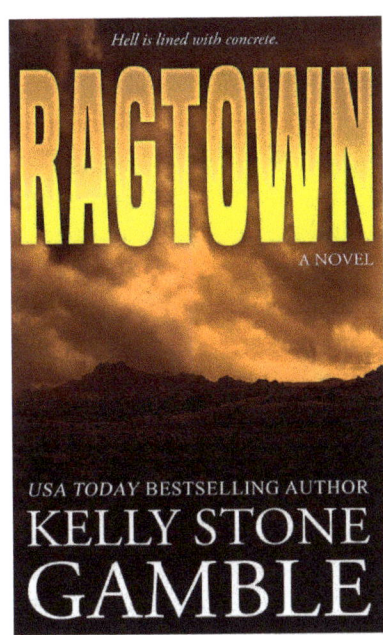

In graduate school, I was fortunate to have Craig Childs as one of my instructors and mentors. Craig, acclaimed for his books set in diverse landscapes, was once dubbed by the New York Times as a "modern-day desert father." Under his guidance, I indeed came to appreciate the allure of the desert, though in an unconventional way. He advised me to engage with the landscape personally - to experience it firsthand. His suggestion? To place a river rock in my mouth, akin to a tobacco plug, and taste the essence of the surroundings. While this initially made no sense to me, I did it. Strangely enough, this experience eventually translated into two pivotal scenes in my book, Ragtown.

When Helen urges Ezra to place a rock in his mouth, she wants him to have the profound connection one establishes with the landscape when engaging with it on an intimate level. Like holding a hay strand between your lips or sipping from a familiar stream, it is a way to become part of the surroundings. In Helen's words, it evokes a sense of home. This newfound perspective allowed her to see the overlooked beauty around her and extended to my own perception.

The desert, mountains, and river are all dynamic, ever-changing, ever-challenging creatures. Once you begin interacting with them as an inhabitant instead of an observer, their magnificence is easy to see. It envelops you, comforts you, and it feels like home.

Writers often visit the settings they will be writing about. In Ragtown, I needed to convey the beauty and peace Helen found around her but also the danger, desperation, and harshness experienced by others who lived in the shadow of Hoover Dam. To do this effectively, I had to do more than just visit; I had to become a part of it temporarily. If that required savoring a rock or two, so be it. Mother Nature opened my world with one taste and gave me what I needed that day: proper understanding.

Kelly Stone Gamble was born in a small Midwestern town and has lived all over the US, including 25 years in Las Vegas, before settling in Tulsa, Oklahoma. Currently a faculty member at Southeastern Oklahoma State University, Kelly shares her passion for literature, the humanities, and writing with aspiring minds. Kelly is the author of the USA Today Bestseller They Call Me Crazy, Call Me Daddy, and Call Me Cass. Her work has appeared in a variety of publications including Red Earth Review, Tower Journal, Family Digest, and Chicken Soup for the Soul and has won awards from Pacific Northwest Writers Association, Writers Weekly, Women on Writing, and the Ground Zero Literary Project.

BRINGING TWO VOICES TOGETHER: AN EDITOR'S POV

Dennis R Bourret and Sam Huynh

I'm not a real publisher; I'm a hybrid publisher who mostly publishes my own work because I'm a meticulous control freak. I'm considering asking my first publisher for permission to redesign the 2nd edition.

I had previously published a collection of Dennis' poetry (<u>Off Highway 20: And Selected Poems</u>). I had created his book for a final project in a publishing class I was taking at the University of Arizona. It was quick and easy, and I charged Dennis a small fee to mostly cover Roman's layout and photography services (Creayto Studios). Everyone was happy.

I really didn't want to take on publishing a narrative book, but after reading both manuscripts, I realized that the world needed to read these stories side by side. There was just so much to gain from these works as one. The book brings the message that we need to find ways to learn from each other no matter the distance.

It took six years of fact-checking at night and on weekends after my regular work hours. I was nervous about Sam's claims and my brainwashed, paranoid American naivety of the Viet Cong. I had to cut whole sections where Sam addressed battle campaigns completely. So, I had to reassure my authors for a very long time and let Sam know how much I was cutting firmly. I also had the task of having to negotiate Sam's English writing as a second language. Sam's writing was beautiful even with so many grammatical hiccups, and I had to fill in the grammatical gaps to maintain its beauty.

What I want you to know as a writer is that if you have a worthy enough story, someone out there will go to great lengths to publish it.

Kelly Stone Gamble was born in a small Midwestern town and has lived all over the US, including 25 years in Las Vegas, before settling in Tulsa, Oklahoma. Currently a faculty member at Southeastern Oklahoma State University, Kelly shares her passion for literature, the humanities, and writing with aspiring minds. Kelly is the author of the USA Today Bestseller They Call Me Crazy, Call Me Daddy, and Call Me Cass. Her work has appeared in a variety of publications including Red Earth Review, Tower Journal, Family Digest, and Chicken Soup for the Soul and has won awards from Pacific Northwest Writers Association, Writers Weekly, Women on Writing, and the Ground Zero Literary Project.

A LATE BLOOMING AUTHOR

Linnea Tanner

I consider myself a late-blooming author. After semi-retiring from the pharmaceutical industry in 2010, I published my first novel, Apollo's Raven, in 2017. Even so, I've passionately read about ancient civilizations and mythology. Since childhood, imaginary characters have lived in my head and told me about their stories. One is a female warrior reminiscent of an Amazon from Greek mythology. Another character is her Roman lover, a military commander. As I faced challenges in my own life, so did my imaginary characters whose tales evolved throughout my adulthood.

In retrospect, creating stories was a way for me to deal with challenges in my own personal life and career. I once admitted to a scientific colleague that I imagined stories in my head and asked if she also did. She answered with a look that reminded me that normal people don't keep imaginary friends past childhood.

Not so for authors, I fortunately discovered. Authors have childlike wonder and imagination. Stories triggered by memories, images, or news on the airways continually weave in and out of their heads. Storytelling is an author's DNA and can be used as a lens to view the world differently. Based on my journey as an author, the following is advice that I would give a writer just starting:

· Write passionately about what interests you, not what is popular.

· Learn your craft by taking workshops, interacting with other writers, and reading stories from other authors in your genre.

· Be open to constructive criticism, but do not let negative comments bring you down.

· Routinely write and finish your first ugly rough draft, then polish and edit.

· Be resilient and never give up.

Award-winning author Linnea Tanner weaves Celtic tales of love, magical adventure, and political intrigue in Ancient Rome and Britannia. She has extensively researched ancient history, mythology, and archaeology and has traveled to sites described in the Curse of Clansmen and Kings series. Books released in her series include Apollo's Raven (Book 1), Dagger's Destiny (Book 2), Amulet's Rapture (Book 3), and Skull's Vengeance (Book 4). A Colorado native, Linnea attended the University of Colorado and earned her BA and MS degrees in chemistry. She lives in Fort Collins with her husband and has two children and six grandchildren.

DEMONSLAYER
Ian P. Eviston

Reviewer: Jeyran Main

"Demonslayer" by Ian P. Eviston is an enthralling fantasy adventure that seamlessly combines elements of magic, conflict, and character development. Set in a world where the mystical substance Aether is pivotal, the story weaves a rich tapestry of a universe where humans and demons coexist, albeit in a tumultuous manner.

The novel's premise revolves around Aether, an essence that resides in every living thing and grants certain humans the power to manipulate elements like fire, water, air, stone, shadow, nature, and metal. This classification of humans into titans, summoners, and enchanters, as well as the concept of high-ranking demons who can manipulate all elements, sets an intriguing foundation for the story.

The central characters, Emily and Spirit Clayborn, are exceptionally crafted. Their journey from struggling on the streets to discovering their Aether abilities is both captivating and emotionally resonant. Spirit's induction into the Vanguard, a legion of humans skilled in using Aether to protect humanity, marks a turning point in the story, escalating the stakes and intensity of the narrative.

One of the book's strengths is its vividly described battle scenes, particularly those involving the Vanguard's struggle against a formidable demon army. These sequences are not only well-executed but also highlight the cost of war, adding depth to the narrative. The revelation of Spirit's parents' past deeds and their impact on his life adds layers of intrigue and complexity to the plot.

Eviston's character development is noteworthy, as each character is given a unique voice and backstory, making them relatable and real. The use of mild profanity contributes to the authenticity of the characters, allowing readers to connect with their emotions and struggles. The array of demons, with their distinct names and characteristics, although initially challenging to follow, ultimately enriches the world-building.

The book is a must-read for fans of J.R.R. Tolkien and Piers Anthony, as Eviston's storytelling skills are on par with these legendary authors. The vivid characters, imaginative creatures, and enthralling plot make "Demonslayer" a standout in the fantasy genre. The minor typos present do not detract from the overall quality of the narrative.

Overall, "Demonslayer" is a captivating start to the Vanguard Chronicles, offering a unique blend of magic, adventure, and emotional depth. With its compelling plot and well-developed characters, this book is a promising beginning to what is sure to be an exciting series. I eagerly anticipate the next installment and highly recommend this book to fantasy enthusiasts.

NEITHER SAFE NOR EFFECTIVE (2ND EDITION): THE EVIDENCE AGAINST THE COVID VACCINES

Dr. Colleen Huber

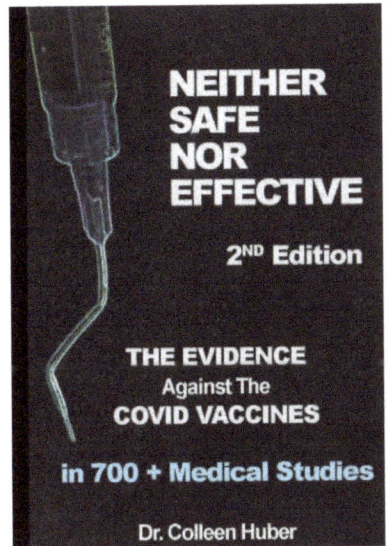

Reviewer: Jeyran Main

In this second edition of "Neither Safe Nor Effective," Dr. Colleen Huber presents a critical examination of the COVID-19 vaccines. The book is structured to provide a comprehensive argument against the use and efficacy of these vaccines, drawing on over 700 references, including medical studies and government web pages. Dr. Huber, who has experience as a medical expert witness in vaccine safety cases, aims to challenge the prevailing narrative surrounding COVID-19 vaccines.

The book asserts that COVID-19 vaccines have resulted in numerous adverse effects, including deaths and injuries, and questions their efficacy in preventing the disease. Dr. Huber describes these vaccines as bioweapons, suggesting they have caused more harm than good. The book discusses various potential health risks associated with the vaccines, such as immune system damage, the development of new cancers, long-term heart and brain damage, DNA alteration, and impaired fertility.

Dr. Huber's approach involves a scientific analysis to scrutinize and challenge the mainstream medical consensus. The book is intended to encourage readers to become independent thinkers, question medical authority, and be wary of what the author perceives as medical tyranny.

It's important for readers to note that the book's content may be controversial and contradicts the consensus of the majority of the medical and scientific community, which generally supports the safety and efficacy of COVID-19 vaccines. Readers are advised to consider multiple sources and consult healthcare professionals when making health-related decisions. Additionally, readers should be aware that the book's claims are a subject of significant debate and scrutiny within the medical community.

LAUNCHPAD REPUBLIC: AMERICA'S ENTREPRENEURIAL EDGE AND WHY IT MATTERS
Howard Wolk, John Landry

Reviewer: Jeyran Main

"Launchpad Republic: America's Entrepreneurial Edge and Why It Matters" by Howard Wolk and John Landry is a comprehensive examination of the American entrepreneurial landscape, its evolution, and its global significance. Drawing on their respective backgrounds as entrepreneurs/investors and business historians/writers, Wolk and Landry delve into the dynamics of the American economic and political system, particularly focusing on the relationship between established companies and emerging startups.

One of the book's strengths is its accessibility. Despite initial concerns about complex language, the authors have presented their ideas clearly and engagingly from the first chapter. This clarity is enhanced by the book's structure, which thoughtfully outlines each chapter's content at the beginning, providing readers with a clear roadmap of the journey ahead.

The authors skillfully utilize storytelling, opening each chapter with relevant anecdotes and historical examples such as A&P, AT&T, and U.S. Steel. These stories captivate the reader and serve as effective analogies for the broader concepts discussed in each chapter.

The depth of research in "Launchpad Republic" is notable, with numerous references to other works and research studies supplemented by charts and data tables for clearer understanding. This meticulous approach underscores the book's credibility and enhances its value as a resource on entrepreneurship.

A key focus of the book is the competition within the entrepreneurial sector, particularly in the American context. The authors explore how the U.S. political, legal, and cultural frameworks have historically enabled entrepreneurs to thrive and innovate, even against powerful competitors. The book also offers comparative analyses with other countries, shedding light on what sets the American entrepreneurial spirit apart.

"Launchpad Republic" is highly recommended for entrepreneurs, business students, and anyone interested in understanding the intricacies of the American economic system and its role in fostering innovation and competition. Its informative and educational content is engaging and enlightening, making it a valuable addition to the literature on entrepreneurship and economic development.

QUEST: FINDING FREDDIE: REFLECTIONS FROM THE OTHER SIDE
Thomas Richard Spradlin

Reviewer: Jeyran Main

"Quest: Finding Freddie: Reflections from the Other Side" by Thomas Richard Spradlin is a gripping historical nonfiction novel that intricately blends adventure, politics, and a deep dive into a rich cultural setting. Set against the tumultuous backdrop of Nigeria in 1976, the book details the author's daring journey to Lagos in search of Frederick David Nachman, a Jewish businessman who mysteriously disappears.

Spradlin's narrative is both captivating and educational, immersing readers in Nigeria's political and social landscape during a critical period in its history. The book provides a fascinating glimpse into the complexities of international relations and the delicate interplay between different governments during a crisis. It's particularly interesting to see how Spradlin navigates the challenges the Swedish and US embassies pose, highlighting the bureaucratic hurdles and diplomatic nuances that often accompany such situations.

The author's descriptive prowess is commendable, bringing to life the vibrant streets of Lagos and the diverse array of characters he encounters. Spradlin's efforts to learn the local vernacular and detailed explanations of Nigerian customs and terms enrich the reading experience, offering a well-rounded portrayal of the country.

One of the book's strengths is its honest depiction of Nigeria during its "glory days," when its economy was more robust and the naira was more substantial than the dollar. This historical insight allows readers to appreciate the drastic changes the country has undergone over the years, adding depth to the narrative.

Spradlin's character development is thorough and meticulous, ensuring that each person he encounters is vividly described. This attention to detail enhances the story's authenticity and helps readers connect with the diverse personalities that populate the narrative.

While the book does contain a few dialogue errors, these do not detract from its overall impact and professional editing. The suspense is well-maintained throughout, making it a compelling read from start to finish.

Overall, "Quest: Finding Freddie" is a remarkable book that deserves a full five out of five stars. It's educational, culturally rich, and suspenseful, making it a perfect choice for readers interested in historical nonfiction, adventure, and political intrigue. The book's immersive storytelling and cultural diversity will captivate and enlighten its audience.

BEYOND THE GOLDEN DOOR: SEEING THE AMERICAN DREAM THROUGH AN IMMIGRANT'S EYES BY ALI MASTER

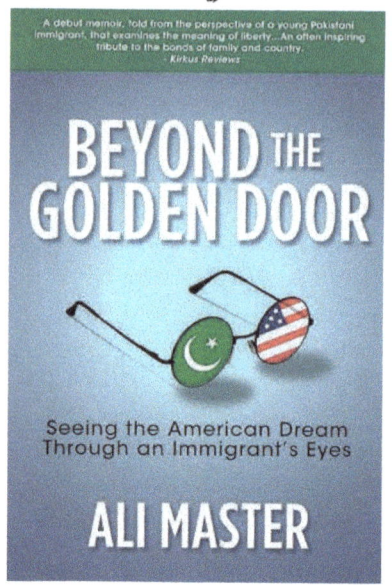

"Beyond the Golden Door" tells the story of Ali Master, a Pakistani Muslim who embarks on a journey to the United States for college, uncovering the true value of freedom through his experiences. In America, he encounters five key freedoms: the ability to fail and start anew, to love, to choose his faith, to pursue entrepreneurship, and to self-govern. These freedoms stand in stark contrast to his life in a developing Muslim country, prompting him to explore their roots and discover that true liberty comes from God. This engaging narrative not only celebrates American liberties but also challenges readers to reflect on their spiritual journey and the ultimate freedom found in Jesus Christ, urging them to cherish and protect these freedoms.

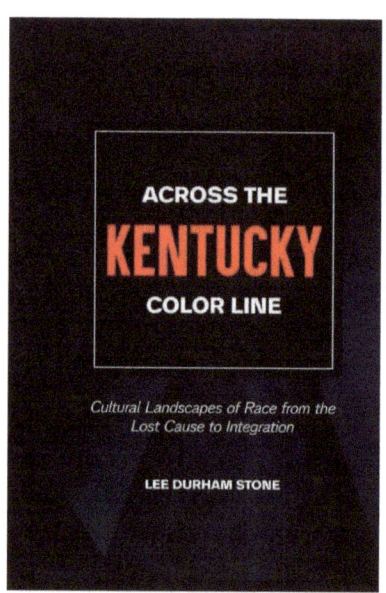

ACROSS THE KENTUCKY COLOR LINE BY LEE DURHAM STONE

This book explores Kentucky's racial history from 1865 to 1970, particularly focusing on Muhlenberg County and its neighbors. It covers post-Civil War racial tensions, the Jim Crow era, Lost Cause politics, and a significant 1907 "legal lynching." The study also examines violence, economic contributions of Black residents, coal mining, involvement in World Wars, and the mysterious suicide of a Black doctor in 1934. It delves into segregated education and the fight for school integration after the 1954 Brown v. Board of Education ruling, concluding with positive developments in the 1970s. The narrative is underpinned by comprehensive research and includes citations for further study.

THE GREAT MIGRATION: BOOK ONE OF THE S'ORNE SAGA BY STEVE RAMIREZ

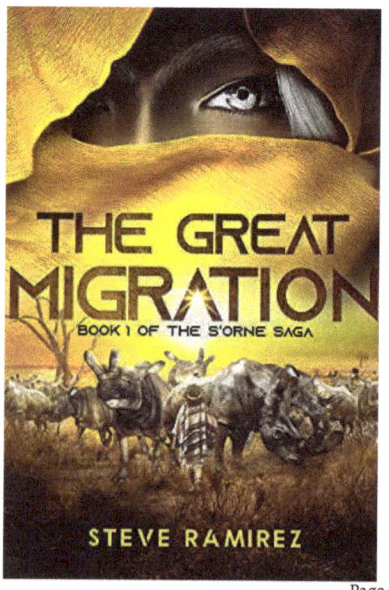

The s'orne, creatures spreading a fever that drives humans to madness, have returned after a century of peace, posing a grave threat to humanity. Bellona, having lived in the wilderness, returns to civilization just as rumors of s'orne attacks begin to spread. During a festival, she uncovers the s'orne's true purpose, challenging her previous beliefs. As the city locks down due to an imminent s'orne attack, Bellona and her friends must flee to avoid the contagion and save their loved ones from the chaos.

www.ingramcontent.com/pod-product-compliance
Lightning Source LLC
Chambersburg PA
CBHW041132120626
46547CB00019B/2963